ARE YOU SICK OF THE DRUM-DRUM-DRUMMING OF
MADISON AVENUE ADS?

CAN YOU TELL WITCH DOCTOR IS WHICH ON
TELEVISION PROGRAMS?

ARE YOU MESMERIZED AND HYPNOTIZED BY
HOLLYWOOD MOVIES?

✳   ✳   ✳   ✳   ✳

**HERE'S YOUR CHANCE TO COME OUT
FROM BEHIND YOUR MASK OF
INDIFFERENCE!**

**HERE'S YOUR OPPORTUNITY TO
STOP SWALLOWING THE SAME OLD
SONG AND DANCE!**

**HERE'S WHERE YOU GET DOWN TO
THE SOURCERY OF ALL YOUR
TROUBLES!**

**MAINLY, YOU ARE ABOUT TO
PRACTICE THAT OLD BLACK-
AND-WHITE MAGIC OF**

THE VOODOO MAD

**. . . AND HAVE YOUR REVENGE BY
STICKING PINS INTO SOME
SACRED COWS! !**

✳   ✳   ✳   ✳   ✳

Ready? Then let's begin!
The first one to get stuck is...YOU!

...FOR BUYING THIS JUNK!

(We just thought we'd needle you a little!)

William M. Gaines's
THE VOODOO
MAD

ALBERT B. FELDSTEIN, Editor

WARNER BOOKS

A Warner Communications Company

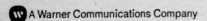

CONTENTS

VIVE LA DIFFERENCE DEPT.

According to Psychologists, most of us clods prefer to follow the "herd instinct

Now and then, however, a few clods with imagination break away from th

Only nowadays, more and more clods are trying to be different, so there a

All except for a small group of bravely idiotic MAD readers — to whom thi

HOW TO BE A

6

—that is, we prefer to think, look and act alike—which makes us all Conformists!

"herd"—and try hard to think, look and act different—which makes them all Non-Conformists!

more and more Non-Conformists! And all the Non-Conformists are so busy conforming to not being Conformists, they all wind up conforming to their Non-Conformism!

article is dedicated—mainly because, in this article, we explain in nauseating detail . . . . .

NON-CONFORMIST

ONLY MAD NON-CONFORMISTS
ACHIEVE GENUINE
ORIGINALITY AS
DEMONSTRATED BY
COMPARING THE HABITS
OF ALL THREE GROUPS

MUSIC

ORDINARY CONFORMISTS

. . . play insipid show scores, dismal pop tunes conducted by Jackie Gleason, sickening dance music by Guy Lombardo, rock n' roll hits by Ricky and Elvis, and occasional works of Gershwin and Tchaikovsky on complicated hi-fi sets.

ORDINARY NON-CONFORMISTS

. . . play obscure folk songs sung by obscure folk, dull chamber music played in dull chambers, Wagnerian operas in their entirety, Gregorian chants, and readings of minor Welsh poets on super-complicated stereo hi-fi sets.

MAD NON-CONFORMISTS

. . . play bird calls, tap dancing and exercise lessons, transcriptions of Senate Committee hearings, Gallagher & Shean, The Singing Lady, and theme music from famous monster movies on easy-to-operate hand-wound victrolas.

MOVIES

ORDINARY CONFORMISTS

. . . go in for uninspired Technicolor musicals, stories with happy endings, migraine-provoking Cinemascope, and 6½-hour double features that destroy the eyes, ears, nose, throat and spine.

ORDINARY NON-CONFORMISTS

. . . patronize stuffy out-of-the-way movie houses that show "experimental" films, arty-type films, documentaries, and obscure foreign language pictures with the sub-titles in pidgin Swahili.

MAD NON-CONFORMISTS

. . . enjoy hand-cranked penny arcade machines which contain film classics like the Dempsey-Firpo fight, Sally Rand's Fan Dance, old Ben Turpin comedies, and Tom Mix pre-adult westerns.

READING

ORDINARY CONFORMISTS

. . . waste their time reading banal best-sellers, trashy whodunits, dull popular magazines, sensational daily newspapers, and commuter time-tables.

ORDINARY NON-CONFORMISTS

. . . go for childish science fiction novels and scientific magazines, arty paperbacks, boring literary journals, and anthologies of avant-garde poetry.

MAD NON-CONFORMISTS

. . . read The Roller Derby News, the pre-Civil War Congressional Record, old Tom Swift books, and back copies of Classified Telephone Directories.

CLOTHING

ORDINARY CONFORMISTS

. . . wear narrow-shouldered charcoal-grey Ivy League suits, button-down. shirts with tight collars, silly caps, cramped Italian style shoes. Females wear Empire dresses and shoes with spike heels that constantly break off.

ORDINARY NON-CONFORMISTS

. . . wear sloppy-looking sweatshirts, grimy blue jeans, arch-crippling sandals, and scratchy beards. Among the females of this group, leotards are usually substituted for blue jeans, and the scratchy beards are optional.

MAD NON-CONFORMISTS

. . . wear smart-looking MAD straight jackets, glamorous opera capes, roomy knickers, comfortable Keds, and lightweight pith helmets which offer good protection in bad weather and provide storage space for day's lichee nuts.

PETS

ORDINARY CONFORMISTS

. . . raise parakeets, cocker spaniels, boxers, collies, turtles, snakes, cats, white mice, parrots and tropical fish.

ORDINARY NON-CONFORMISTS

. . . raise Russian wolfhounds, French poodles, Weimaraners, ocelots, minks, deodorized skunks and rhesus monkeys.

MAD NON-CONFORMISTS

. . . raise ant colonies, anteaters, falcons, leeches, octopii, anchovies, water buffaloes and performing fleas.

FOOD

ORDINARY CONFORMISTS

prefer meals like on menu below.

Sam's
chop house

Tomato Juice
Celery and Olives
Vegetable Soup
Sirloin Steak
Green Peas and Carrots
French Fried Potatoes
Hearts of Lettuce Salad
Apple Pie a la Mode
Coffee

ORDINARY NON-CONFORMISTS

prefer meals like on menu below.

KEROUAC'S
coffee shop

Snails
Sweetbreads
Vichyssoise
Beef Bourguignon
Wild Rice
Pommes de Terre Soufflés
Hearts of Artichoke Salad
Camembert Cheese
Caffé Espresso

MAD NON-CONFORMISTS

prefer meals like on menu below.

Neuman's
way-out house

Hummingbird Tongues
on Toast
Kippered Guppy
Purée of Electric Eel
Flamingo Under Glass
Creamed Crab Grass
Sweet Potato Chips
Hearts of Cactus Salad
Licorice Sherbert
Maxie

END

13

More and more these days, the trend is toward "realism" in entertainment. Take all them TV heroes, for example. Guys like Bat Masterson, Wyatt Earp, and Jack Benny. These characters aren't made up! No sir! They're taken from real life! If newspaper syndicates were smart, they'd get on the ball, follow the trend, and get more realism in their features by using these...

COMIC STRIP HEROES

(TAKEN FROM REAL LIFE)

15

CONRAD HILTON AND HIS HOTELS

WERNER VON BRAUN — SPACE WIZARD

WERNER AND HIS CREW ARE LAUNCHING A ROCKET AIMED AT THE NEBULA IN ANDROMEDA...

...5...4...3...2...1! SHE'S OFF, WERNER! SHE'S ON HER WAY!

ACH! DOT'S GREAT! IMACHIN! 75,000 MILES OF VIRING...300,000 ELECTRICAL CONNECTIONS ...A MILLION CHANCES TO GO WRONG...UND *VE SUCCEED!*

AND WE OWE IT ALL TO *YOU*, WERNER! *YOU* DESIGNED THE ROCKET! *YOU* DESIGNED THE LAUNCHING PAD! *YOU* DESIGNED THIS CONTROL ROOM! *YOU*... ARE A *GENIUS!*

ACH! IT VAS NUTTING!

LET'S TUNE IN THE SHORTWAVE RADIO SO WE CAN HEAR THE ROCKET'S SIGNALS!

ACH! DOT'S A GOOT IDEA! I WILL PLUG IT IN UND... UND... *HIMMEL!* VAS IST LOHS!?

MILTOWN PRODINGS SICILY

WERNER? IS THERE SOMETHING WRONG WITH THE *ROCKET?*

ACH! NO! VOT IS WRONG IS VIT DER *RADIO!* IT IS *AC*... UND DER CONTROL ROOM IS *DC!*

BRINGING UP BONNIE PRINCE CHARLIE

HYMIE RICKOVER AND HIS ATOMIC SUBS

WELL, ADMIRAL RICKOVER! THERE GOES THE *SIXTH ATOMIC SUB*... DOWN THE WAYS!

YES, IT *IS* AN IMPRESSIVE SIGHT, ISN'T IT?

YOU MUST FEEL MIGHTY *PROUD*... SEEING ALL YOUR DREAMS AND PLANS AND THE THINGS YOU FOUGHT FOR BECAUSE YOU BELIEVED IN THEM COMING TRUE!

YES, IT WAS MIGHTY *TOUGH GOING* THERE FOR A WHILE!

TELL ME, ADMIRAL! WHAT DOES IT *FEEL* LIKE WHEN YOU'RE DOWN IN AN ATOMIC SUB?

HOW SHOULD *I* KNOW?

YOU MEAN... YOU'VE NEVER BEEN *DOWN* IN AN ATOMIC SUB?

THAT'S *RIGHT!* MAINLY BECAUSE I'VE NEVER BEEN *INVITED!*

WOODROW UNDERWOOD WOOD.

DICK NIXON IN WASHINGTON

NASSER AND THE ARABS

WHAT'S WRONG, GAMEL? YOU LOOK *UNHAPPY!*

I *AM!* TITO AND FRANCO HAVE INVITED ME TO THE DICTATOR'S DANCE, BUT I *CAN'T GO!* THERE'S NO *MONEY* IN OUR TREASURY!

WAIT! I'VE GOT AN *IDEA!*

HELLO... IS THIS THE *AMERICAN AMBASSADOR?* I NEED A MILLION DOLLARS! IF I DON'T GET IT RIGHT AWAY, I'LL GO *COMMUNIST!* FINE! SEND IT RIGHT OVER...

NOW.. ANOTHER PHONE CALL...

HELLO... IS THIS THE *RUSSIAN AMBASSADOR?* I NEED A MILLION RUBLES! IF I DON'T GET IT RIGHT AWAY, I'LL JOIN THE *PRO-WESTERN BAGHDAD PACT!* GREAT! SEND IT RIGHT OVER...

YOU'RE A GENIUS, GAMEL! *A GENIUS!* NOW YOU CAN GO TO THE DICTATOR'S DANCE!

I SURE CAN! HEH-HEH! JUST WAIT TILL I TELL TITO AND FRANCO ABOUT *THIS!* THEY'LL FLIP...

THE KHRUSHCHEVS

HOFFA THE MENACE

"Kid, what you need is a union! You look
like somebody wit' a lot of grievances!"

END

I must go down in the sea again, down deep, cause I'm in the mood...
And all I ask is my air should last, so I don't end up fish food!
John Masefinkle—Skin Diver from Hackensack

IN THE OLD DAYS, THE MORE ADVENTUROUS SOULS AMONG US USED TO DREAM OF GOING DOWN TO THE SEA IN SHIPS. NOWADAYS, THE

SKIN

Scientists tell us that life on Earth can be traced back millions of years . . . to its origin in the sea around us. There, the first one-celled animal bobbed, then wriggled

MORE ADVENTUROUS SOULS AMONG US DREAM
OF GOING DOWN TO THE SEA . . . AND THEN
UNDER IT . . .

DIVING

THE SATELLITE SEEN IN THE UPPER RIGHT CONTAINS SEVERAL COWS. IT IS THE
FIRST HERD SHOT 'ROUND THE WORLD!

then swam, and finally crawled onto land to develop into
the creature known as "Man". Yes, through the process of
evolution, we have come a long way upward . . . ever upward

This article deals with the reactionaries to this evolution. Mainly, the skin divers who are reversing the process by returning to the sea and going downward, ever downward. This, then, is an article with depth.

To accomplish this return to the sea, skin divers must have the special equipment shown below: (1) Face Mask, (2) Oxygen Tank, (3) Rubber Suit, (4) Weighted Belt, (5) Flippers, (6) Wrist Depth Gauge, (7) Spear, and (8) Knife. Manufacturers who supply this equipment charge fantastic prices for it, proving there's more than one way to skin a skin diver!

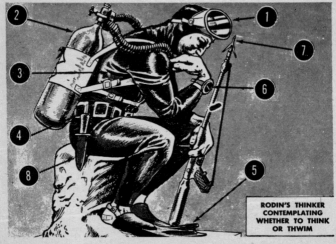

RODIN'S THINKER CONTEMPLATING WHETHER TO THINK OR THWIM

SKIN DIVING ENTHUSIASTS CLAIM THEY CAN ENJOY MANY FACETS OF THE SPORT

SALVAGE

Skin diving enthusiasts claim they derive enjoyment from searching for and finding lost valuables they can salvage.

OBSERVATION

Skin diving enthusiasts claim there's lots of thrills and plenty excitement studying forms of marine life close-up.

DISCOVERY

Skin diving enthusiasts claim nothing can match the eerie mystery of discovering and investigating old sunken hulks.

EXPLORATION

Skin diving enthusiasts claim once you've experienced the dangers of exploring undersea caves, you've really lived.

Spear-fishing is popular among the more bloodthirsty skin divers. Spears used in this delightful sport come in the many and varied types shown above, all designed to KILL!

Skin divers will tell you that spear-fishing is far more thrilling than rod-and-reel fishing . . . and that once you have experienced it, your thirst for it is unquenchable!

FISHING

While a rod-and-reel fisherman must wait patiently for a hungry fish to take his bait, the skin diver with a spear can go below and plaster one whether it's hungry or not!

An expert skin diver never goes spear-fishing alone, but uses the safer "buddy system"...the advantage being that if there are no fish to shoot, there's always his "buddy"!

THE UNDERWATER CAMERA

The development of water-tight casings for cameras opened a new world for skin divers, while landlubber photo bugs were stuck on shore with the same old mundane subjects.

MAD shudders to think what will happen if skin diving continues to gain in popularity. Before long, this return to the sea . . . this reversal of the evolutionary process

DEVELOPMENTS

THE AQUA-LUNG

The development of the aqua-lung made it possible for the skin diver to remain underwater longer, breathing air at $5.00 a tankful which he can get above water for FREE!

. . . will begin to have its effects, and once again, Man will develop gills, then scales, then fins, until finally he ends up as that wriggling, bobbing, one-celled animal.

END

NOW THAT SUMMER IS APPROACHING, WITH IT'S HEAT AND HUMIDITY, IT'S

MIRACLE

Today's miracle fabrics are woven from specially-treated, or synthetic yarns. The finished products eliminate many problems, and at the same time increase the comforts of the wearers. There are three main selling-points offered

WASH N' WEAR...

On important business trip, busy executive is unworried when mud splashes on his suit as he arrives at airport.

FABRICS

by miracle fabrics: (1) Wash 'n Wear, (2) Wrinkleproof, and (3) Stretchable. The purpose of this article is to demonstrate these three main selling points, and thereby illustrate the wonderful *advantages* of miracle fabrics.

One suit serves every need

At hotel, he scrubs suit while bathing, saving money and worry over not getting it back from the cleaners in time.

...A boon to busy executives,

Sudden downpour on way to important business conference does not faze carefree executive in "Wash 'n wear" suit.

At conference, neat-looking executive shivers, not from nervousness, but from chill of wet suit drying on body.

lazy slobs, and cheapskates.

Arriving in building lobby, drenched businessman finds fan . . . and suit is dried as good as new in 15 minutes.

Slight chill of previous day causes slight cold, so busy executive stays in bed. Note suit now serves as pajamas.

Slight complication develops from slight cold caused by slight chill which leads to slight case of pneumonia, and

WRINKLEPROOF..

...A boon to those who have

ORDINARY

In crowded subway train, woman wears ordinary cloth dres

"Wash 'n wear" suit sees still further use, proving that miracle fabrics not only look good, but last a lifetime!

Stands stress and strain
to pack and unpack every day.

CLOTH

When she leaves, ordinary cloth dress is badly wrinkled.

In crowded subway train, woman wears miracle fabric dress.

MIRACLE FABRIC

FABRIC

When she leaves, her miracle fabric dress is unwrinkled.

CLOTHES THAT...

Stretch leotard made to fit everyone, in original unstretched single size.

Three-year-old toddler fitted snugly. Fabric hardly stretches at all.

DEMONSTRATION OF IMPORTANT ADVANTAGE

STRETCH SOCK ... HUNG UP ON CHRISTMAS EVE

STRETCH ITEM SIZE FITS EVERYONE!

Ten-year-old youngster also fitted well. Fabric shows slight stretching.

20-year-old girl fitted the best of all! Fabric really shows stretching!

DISCOVERED BY KIDS LAST XMAS!

STRETCH SOCK . . . FULL UP CHRISTMAS MORNING

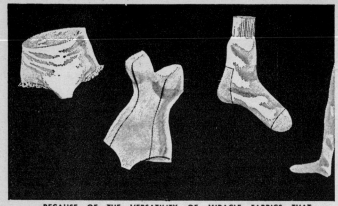

BECAUSE OF THE VERSATILITY OF MIRACLE FABRICS THAT
MATERIAL ARE APPEARING ON THE MARKET. PICTURED ABOVE
(Note that items illustrated are actual

DEMONSTRATION OF HOW ONE STRETCH

Unstretched underwear
worn as cool briefs in
blistering Summer heat.

Slightly-stretched, can
be worn as comfortable
shorts in balmy Spring.

STRETCH, MORE AND MORE ARTICLES OF APPAREL MADE FROM THIS ARE SOME OF THE REMARKABLE STRETCH ITEMS AVAILABLE TODAY size, but will stretch to fit anybody!)

ITEM ADJUSTS TO YEAR-ROUND WEAR!

Stretched a little more, affords warmth needed in brisk Fall weather.

Stretched all the way, affords protection in frigid Winter weather.

DEMONSTRATION OF IMPORTANT DISADVANTAGE INHERENT IN STRETCH ITEMS!

Stretch fabrics, like bathing suits, are always under extreme tension...

... which, when suddenly released ...

... snap back to their original size!

END

In a recent MAD article (*Body-Building & Weight Lifting*, No. 45.), valuable information was given on a program for keeping fit through exercise. Unfortunately, the average person has neither the equipment, knowledge, nor incentive to carry through such a program. Today, all these objections are being solved by a dedicated young health expert. This young health expert is dedicated to making Americans healthy. The money he's making ($15,000,000 a year) is of secondary importance to him. He's only interested (he says!) in getting every single man, woman and child into

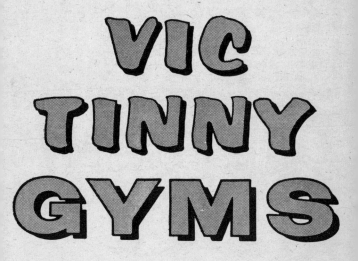

VIC TINNY GYMS

A PUBLIC SERVICE TO IMPROVE AMERICA'S HEALTH

When Vic Tinny started his dedicated campaign to make all America healthy, he was faced with a huge problem: how to

Old-style gyms were dark, dingy, and worst of all, they smelled like dirty sweatsocks!

VIC TINNY GYMS ARE SHINY, BRIGHT, AND BEST

get people into a gym? Old-style gyms were unappealing! Vic's answer: The completely-redesigned "Vic Tinny Gym."

OF ALL, THEY SMELL LIKE **CLEAN** SWEATSOCKS!

THE NEW VIC TINNY METHOD

POPULAR HEALTH METHODS WHICH
DIET METHOD

DIET METHOD alone loses weight all over body, even in places that were all right as they were.

Before going ahead with his dedicated campaign, Vic Tinny examined many other "health methods." He discovered that people needed three things to successfully complete them: (1) Instruction, (2) Equipment, and (3) Incentive. After months of planning, Vic came up with the "Tinny Method": (1) Instruction, (2) Equipment, and (3) Iron-clad Contract. When a Vic Tinny student realizes how much it is costing for every minute he's in the gym, he exercises like crazy!

VIC TINNY FOUND INADEQUATE

found inadequate

DIET METHOD alone removes fat, but skin stays same size, and with no fat below, sags all over.

EXERCISE METHOD alone develops only the muscles that are exercised, often with very weird results.

EQUIPMENT METHOD

EQUIPMENT METHOD alone is inadequate because soft-

EXERCISE METHOD alone develops huge appetite, subsequent over-eating, and unwanted new muscles.

living public is too far gone for machines to help.

VIC TINNY'S HEALTH METHOD COM

DIET: VIC TINNY'S PROVIDES FACILITIES DISPENSING

EXERCISE: VIC TINNY'S PROVIDES STAFF OF SPECIAL

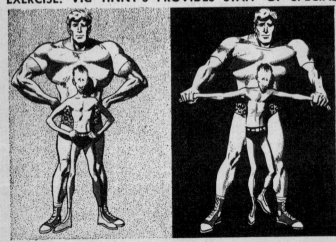

BINES BEST FEATURES OF ALL

SPECIAL HEALTH FOODS.

LY-TRAINED INSTRUCTORS.

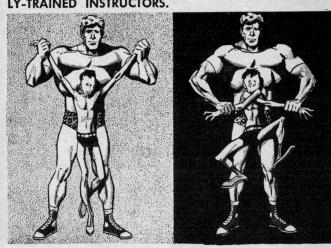

SPECIAL PROBLEMS

SPECIAL HEALTH PROBLEMS ARE HANDLED WITH PRECISION AND KNOW-HOW AT VIC TINNY'S

Man has special arms and legs problem.

Skilled Vic Tinny Experts go to work.

Man ends up with perfect proportions.

SOME OTHER
REMARKABLE CASE HISTORIES,
ANALYZED AND SOLVED
BY VIC TINNY EXPERTS

PROBLEM: Woman's head too small for her body.

PROBLEM: Woman's figure prevented movie career.

SOLVED
by
Vic Tinny Gyms, Inc.

PROBLEM: Woman's husband refused to be seen with her.

SOLVED
by
Vic Tinny Gyms, Inc.

THE BUS

One word describes the Vic Tinny operation: "efficiency". As soon as a person steps into a Vic Tinny Gym, he is immediately impressed with this efficiency. Before he has a chance to say, "I came in for a free figure analysis like you advertised!" he has signed a 12-year contract, had his clothes removed, and is flying up and down on a power-driven see-saw. It's this kind of efficiency that has brought 180,000 signed-up cus-

AS A NEW GYM OPENS EVERY 13 MINUTES

tomers into Vic Tinny Gyms, even some they never expected, like little old ladies asking directions or looking for rest rooms. Yes, efficiency has created a nationwide chain of successful Vic Tinny Gyms. Work to improve this efficiency never ends. In fact, it is hoped that someday it may reach the "Health Improvement" Department.

THE ULTIMATE DREAM

Vic Tinny says:

"Someday, I hope to see every man, woman, and child in this great big wonderful world of ours enjoying all the benefits and advantages of good health that the Vic Tinny Method of exercise can bring to them!"

Vic Tinny's own "method" of exercising for his health.

Some people remember their early childhood years as being happy. Others remember them as being unhappy.

HOW TO PLAY

on Martin can't recall his early childhood years at
! Not after the time his big brother taught him...

CROQUET

END

Announcing...

THE
GREATEST
MISSILE
EVER
BUILT

With this article, MAD scoops all other leading scientific publications and lifts the veil of secrecy on a fantastic new missile now being readied for its final test. (Unfortunately, we are not at liberty to reveal which nation has this ultimate weapon, but that sort of adds to the excitement!)

WHY THIS MISSILE WAS DEVELOPED

Pictures of present day ordinary missiles show need for new approach

WHEN PRESENT-DAY ORDINARY MISSILE IS LAUNCHED, IT FLIES THROUGH EARTH'S ATMOSPHERE

IN ATMOSPHERE, ORDINARY MISSILE IS EASILY DETECTED ELECTRONICALLY BY ENEMY DEFENSES

ONCE IT IS DETECTED, ENEMY DEFENSES IMMEDIATELY LAUNCH SPECIAL INTERCEPTOR MISSILE

ENEMY INTERCEPTOR MISSILE BLOWS UP ORDINARY $3,000,000 MISSILE, CAUSING GREAT WASTE

THEREFORE, SCIENCE WAS FACED WITH PROBLEM OF DEVELOPING UNDETECTABLE MISSILE! FOR SUCCESSFUL RESULTS, TURN PAGE:

GREATEST MISSILE EVER BUILT BLASTS RIGHT CLEAR THROUGH THE EARTH!

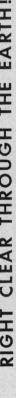

SIMPLY AIM IT ANYWHERE!

The Inner Space Guided Missile is simplicity itself. All that is necessary is to decide upon the country you want to blow off the face of the Earth, calculate the aim, and fire!

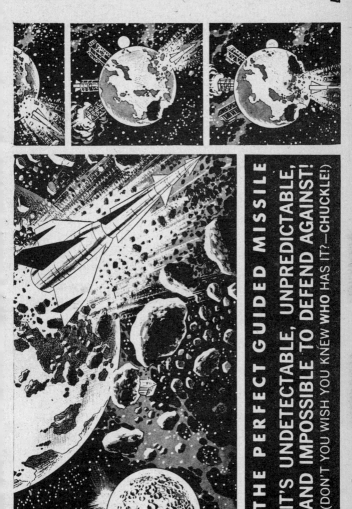

THE PERFECT GUIDED MISSILE

IT'S UNDETECTABLE, UNPREDICTABLE, AND IMPOSSIBLE TO DEFEND AGAINST!

(DON'T YOU WISH YOU KNEW WHO HAS IT?—CHUCKLE!)

Anxious to keep our grimy thumb on the pulse of the American public, we recently took a trip around the country. And everywhere we went, we heard the same thing. Mainly, "Get outa town, yuh bums!" However, we also heard people grumbling about modern cars. Tailfins are higher, wheel bases are longer, and tempers are shorter. Hoping to be of help, MAD took a nationwide poll, asking people what changes they wanted—and here are the results of that poll. Using a composite model of typical American cars, we've indicated below what the public wants included in . . .

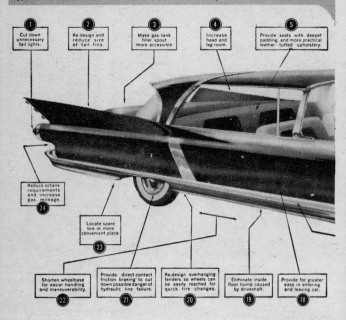

1 Cut down unnecessary tail lights.

2 Re-design and reduce size of tail fins.

3 Make gas tank filler spout more accessible

4 Increase head and leg room.

5 Provide seats with deeper padding, and more practical leather tufted upholstery.

24 Reduce octane requirements and increase gas mileage.

23 Locate spare tire in more convenient place.

22 Shorten wheelbase for easier handling and maneuverability.

21 Provide direct-contact friction braking to cut down possible danger of hydraulic line failure.

20 Re-design overhanging fenders so wheels can be easily reached for quick tire changes.

19 Eliminate inside floor hump caused by driveshaft.

18 Provide for greater ease in entering and leaving car.

AMERICA'S DREAM CAR

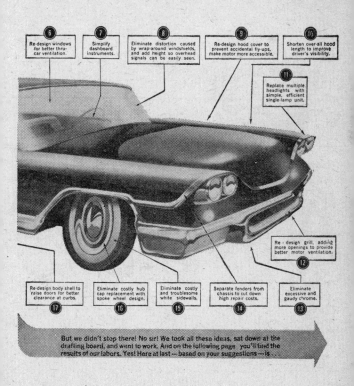

6 Re-design windows for better thru-car ventilation.

7 Simplify dashboard instruments.

8 Eliminate distortion caused by wrap-around windshields, and add height so overhead signals can be easily seen.

9 Re-design hood cover to prevent accidental fly-ups, make motor more accessible.

10 Shorten over-all hood length to improve driver's visibility.

11 Replace multiple headlights with simple, efficient single-lamp unit.

12 Re-design grill, adding more openings to provide better motor ventilation.

17 Re-design body shell to raise doors for better clearance at curbs.

16 Eliminate costly hub cap replacement with spoke wheel design.

15 Eliminate costly and troublesome white sidewalls.

14 Separate fenders from chassis to cut down high repair costs.

13 Eliminate excessive and gaudy chrome.

But we didn't stop there! No sir! We took all these ideas, sat down at the drafting board, and went to work. And on the following page you'll find the results of our labors. Yes! Here at last — based on your suggestions — is . . .

AMERICA'S
DREAM CAR

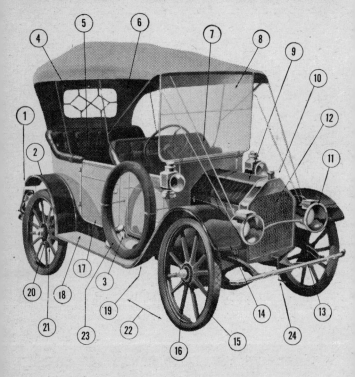

END

Every single Saturday night for the past two years on TV, master sleuth and legal eagle, Perry Masonmint, has outwitted District Attorney Hamilton Burgerbits. Now, we don't know if this poor schnook of a DA ever wins any cases during the week, but we certainly think it would be a refreshing change if, just for once, we could turn on our television set and watch . . .

THE NIGHT THAT

PERRY MASONMINT

LOST A CASE

78

Paul, grab a plane to Cooperstown . . . to the Baseball Hall of Fame . . . check the archives, and find out how many home runs **Rogers Hornsby** hit in **Yankee Stadium** in his major league career!

Right, Perry! I'll be back soon . . .

Your Honor . . . I have here a copy of the 1958 American League baseball schedule, which proves conclusively that on April 14, the day of the murder, the **N. Y. Yankees** were playing in **Kansas City!**

I object! If Mr. Masonmint is right, then perhaps he can tell me what seventy-thousand people were **doing** in Yankee Stadium that day?

That he tried to kill Della Sweet because she knew too much . . . That he sent Paul Dreck on a wild goose chase to get him out of this courtroom . . . and that this morning, he married the defendant, Harry Townes, so Harry couldn't testify against him!

Mr. Masonmint, do you know why 70,000 fans were in Yankee Stadium on a day when the Yankees were in Kansas City? I'll tell you why! I invited them there! I wanted them to witness that murder! They're all personal friends of mine, and I intend to call each and every one of them to the stand to testify! I'm going to convict you, Masonmint, if it takes a lifetime! Mr. Bailiff . . . start calling these witnesses to the stand in alphabetical order . . .

Anthony A. Aardvark, take the stand, please!

END

FUN FOR THE ROAD DEPT.

Some people claim that billboards are ugly and should be taken down. Other people say that billboards blot out pretty scenery and should be taken down. As far as MAD'S concerned, we say "Leave 'em up!" Because those billboards can be very funny! Especially when a new advertisement is being pasted over an old one... and parts of the two signs can be seen at the same time. Like f'rinstance, these...

Half-finished
BILLBOARDS

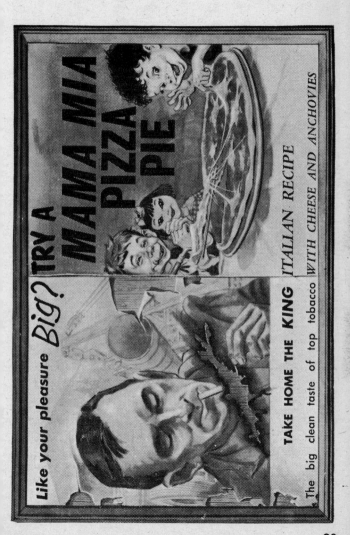

Like your pleasure *Big?* TRY A

MAMA MIA PIZZA PIE

ITALIAN RECIPE WITH CHEESE AND ANCHOVIES

TAKE HOME THE KING

The big clean taste of top tobacco

94

Everywhere we look these days, we see posters publicizing well-known progressive organizations and their constructive campaigns. Nowhere do we see posters publicizing little-known reactionary or-

LITTLE KNOWN

Join The Crusade To Abolish The Arts!

Music, Art, Literature and the Drama are ruining our great nation by encouraging us to escape from the stark realities of life. Too much time and money are wasted on such dangerous frivolities. We must wake up before it is too late and use this time and money for something really worthwhile, or face ultimate destruction!

Participate In Our Many Important Activities

Join "Send Artists To The Moon" Clubs — Support Book-Burning Demonstrations—Break up Poetry Readings —Talk Loud in Libraries—Cough at Symphony Concerts

Picket Art Wherever It's Found!

MUSEUMS   GALLERIES   STUDIOS   REST ROOM WALLS

The Anti-Cultural League

This month's drive to destroy Culture is devoted to: "Making the Country MAD Conscious"

ganizations and their destructive campaigns. Since we at MAD believe that everybody has the right to be heard, here are some appeals for support from...

ORGANIZATIONS

Wipe Out
CORRUPTION in GOVERNMENT
by Wiping Out GOVERNMENT!
GIVE GOVERNMENT BACK TO THE PEOPLE!
MAKE EVERYBODY HIS OWN LAWMAKER!

Let's return to Rugged Individualism!

DON'T VOTE ON ELECTION DAY!

DON'T SUPPORT POLITICAL PARTIES!

DON'T OBEY THE LAWS OF THE LAND!

DON'T EVEN JOIN THIS ORGANIZATION!

Americans for **D**emocratic **A**narchy

An Organization Dedicated to the Proposition that "Government Stinks!"

BACK BLIGHT

PROTEST AGAINST THE TEARING DOWN OF OUR-BELOVED TENEMENTS FOR BIG HOUSING PROJECTS THAT DRIVE US FURTHER INTO CONFORMITY!

ACTION

American Committee To Ignore Our Neighborhoods

Consult your Yellow Pages under "SLOBS" for the office nearest you!

Keep Our Communities Looking Lived In!

* THROW TRASH IN HALLWAYS
* DESTROY WASTE-DISPOSAL UNITS
* JOIN HOUSE-WRECKING DEMONSTRATIONS
* ATTACK YOUR STREET CLEANER WHEN HE COMES

Special Committees now being formed to bring back:

* PUSHCARTS
* OUTDOOR CLOTHES-LINES
* KITCHEN DUMBWAITERS
* THE "I-CASH-CLOTHES" MAN

SEND FOR FREE 1-PAGE BOOKLET
"How To Turn Your Neighborhood Into A Slum Area."

JOIN **ACTION** TODAY!

INDIVIDUALISM NATURALISM CHARACTER

A S P C A

American
Society for the
Practice of
Cruelty to
Animals

BRING YOUR PET TO ONE OF OUR CONVENIENTLY LOCATED TORTURE CHAMBERS

OUR MOTTO: Get them before they get you!

It's time to fight back!

123,497
People bitten by DOGS last year

15,382
Individuals scratched by CATS last month

5,289
Women frightened by MICE last week

1
Clod smacked by an ELEPHANT'S TRUNK last night

ENTER OUR EXCITING NEW CONTEST "The most vicious cruelty to a Domestic Animal"

Why Not Direct Natural Human Aggression Against Animals Instead Of Each Other?

THEY'RE DOING IT TO US!

- Go out and kick dogs in the gut!
- Set fire to stray kittens!
- Pull wings off flies!
- Tape the beaks of annoying parakeets!
- Pluck feathers off live chickens!
- Walk around stepping on ants!

ALCOHOLICS!

If you're going to drink . . . Why not get drunk among friends!

Nobody understands a drunk better than another drunk! Here is a place you can come where nobody's going to try and make you kick the habit!

FOR OLD TIMERS

Meet other drunks with the same neurosis as yours!

Make new friends and life-long drinking companions!

FOR BEGINNERS

Special courses on "How to become a Confirmed Alcoholic"

"How to convert your friends into Confirmed Alcoholics"

Join the only Organization of Active Lushes in America

Alcoholics Unanimous!

"A HOME AWAY FROM THE SALOON"

("Just knock three times and holler: "A. U.!")

SPECIAL FIELD TRIPS TO BOTTLE CLUBS, MOONSHINE STILLS, AND SKID ROW HOTELS

Help Stamp Out
Togetherness

"Togetherness" is ruining America! Members of families are getting into each other's hair! Arguments are starting! Fights are common! It's time to stop this Threat to America's Future! Stay apart and preserve our homes!

JOIN CAMPAIGNS FOR:
* SEPARATE BEDROOMS
* SEPARATE VACATIONS
* SEPARATE AUTOMOBILES
* SEPARATE CHECKS
* SEPARATE COPIES OF "McCALLS"

Enroll Today In The
UNTOGETHERNESS CLUB OF AMERICA

Executive Office....................Toledo, Ohio
Administrative Office........Dubuque, Iowa
Editorial Office........Fargo, North Dakota
Meeting Rooms..............Sydney, Australia

DON'T FIGHT
JUVENILE DELINQUENCY
JOIN IT!

Stop being a sissy! Get out of the house! Take part in friendly neighborhood skirmishes! Prepare yourself for the rough adult life you will have to face tomorrow!

**FOR THE RELEASE OF
PENT-UP HOSTILITY
JOIN A STREET
GANG TODAY!**

*Make it the best Fighting Force
in your Local Community!*

LEARN GOOD TRADES
FOR THE FUTURE:

—Sew patches on black leather jackets!
—Learn to sharpen switchblade knives!
—Become adept at polishing brass knuckles!
—Master the art of dirty fighting!
—Get used to being knocked around!

Committee to Encourage
Juvenile Delinquency

A Non-Profit Organization
Sponsored by the

Police Antagonistic League
OUR MOTTO:
**"Don't send your boy to Camp—
send him to Reform School!"**

Clarke

Support this Revolutionary New Way to Solve the Overpopulation Problem!

Have an Accident TODAY!

Let's face it! You've got to go eventually so you might as well go fast! Why wait for lingering disease or slow, tormenting old age? Let us show you how to have a quick, easy accident!

ATTEND OUR ENTERTAINING WEEKLY LECTURES:

MAY 5:
"Forming a Self-Destructive Group Among Your Friends."

MAY 12:
"101 Ways to Get Yourself Killed In Your Home"

MAY 19:
"How to Take Better Advantage of Heavy Traffic."

MAY 26:
"Live Wires, Third Rails and Where to Find Them."

PHONE OR WRITE **N**ational **A**ccident **C**ouncil

"Don't have an Accident without first consulting us!"

END

103

MAD's maddest artist, Don Martin, who firmly believes in protecting America's Wild Life (mainly because it's the only life he knows) now relates the tale of . . .

THE
FISHERMEN

END

HONESTLY THIS IS THE BEST POLICY DEPT.

Every now and then we get an irritating phone call from an irritating man with an irritating voice who tries to sell us insurance. The irritating thing is . . . we always buy some! At present, we're insured against fire, flood, famine, theft, loss, tornadoes, beri-beri, and being crushed to death by a stampede of elephants while walking East on 28th Street between 2 and 4

FURD-AMERICAN
CASUALTY CO.

BLIND DATE

INSURANCE

This policy provides cash compensation in the event that the insured (hereinafter referred to as "the insured") should be unwittingly trapped into a blind date with an undesirable, unpleasant or disgusting type person (hereinafter referred to as "disgusting type person".)

FURD-AMERICAN
"The Insurancier Insurance"

This policy will be revoked if the insured is unable to read this paragraph from 200 yards without glasses.

a.m. So, now that the insurance people have us grown-up clods insured up to the ears, why don't they start pestering the teen-age set? Most teen-agers have big problems and they need insurance! Also, most teen-agers have big money and they can afford it! To get the ball rolling, MAD opens a new field for the leading Insurance Companies of America with these ...

INSURANCE POLICIES FOR TEEN-AGERS

PARAGRAPH 14—Sub section 3.b

Cash payments to either sex per this policy will be determined by the kind of blind date involved, in accordance with the following standard Furd-American actuarial table:

BLIND DATE TYPE	PAYMENT
Bore	$ .75
Goon	1.05
Clod	1.72
Mama's Baby	2.50
Wolf	2.98
Gargoyle	4.00
Creature from the Black Lagoon	6.75
Alfred E. Neuman	50.00

PARAGRAPH 23-Sub-sub section K

When requesting payment, claimant must supply photo of blind date, and detailed information as indicated:

NAME OF DATE, IF ANY _____

PLACE OF DATE, IF ANY _____

COLOR OF DATE'S HAIR, IF ANY _____

attach blind date's photo here

WHAT NAUSEATED YOU THE MOST ABOUT THIS PARTICULAR PERSON? _____

_____

WHY? _____

INEQUITABLE BENEFIT

INSURANCE COMPANY
Rockrib, Maine

𝕱lunk

INSURANCE

This policy will remain in force until graduation of the Insured. It provides payment for all the courses failed by the Insured, and for suitable coverage on examinations, quizzes and tests as hereinafter stated.

Eugene St. Jean

Sec'y

POLICY NO. 22736 B - 09

"IF IT'S OURS, IT'S INEQUITABLE"

This policy, although it is designed for teen-agers, shall be declared null and void if sold to a minor.

SECTION 2395—

If claimant fails to pass final exams as specified, the Company agrees to pay the sum of one dollar ($1) for every point below passing grade. For grades under 40, compensation is increased to two dollars ($2). For all grades under 20, claimant receives a free transfer to another school.

SECTION 4693—

Before receiving any cash benefit the claimant must file an affidavit certifying that he or she has made every effort to pass. CAUTION: *honest effort is not enough!* The Claimant must furnish proof that he or she attempted to *cheat* whenever and wherever possible, and to *purchase answers* from brighter, non-insured classmates.

AXOLOTL
BENEVOLENT ASSOCIATION

MAKE-OUT
INSURANCE

E Pluribus Axolotl

In accordance with the provisions stated herein, this policy guarantees refund of all money spent on heavy dates where insured does not succeed in making out.

Extra payment is provided in cases where the claimant not only fails to make out but sustains bodily injury.

POLICY NO. 553.77

PARAGRAPH 43—

The Company hereby agrees to refund amounts spent on heavy dates (plus 10%) in all cases where valid proof can be presented that claimants date walked home from car ride, slapped his face in the movies, or otherwise refused to cooperate.

RIDER NO. 17-c—

Additional cash bonus will be paid where claimant's efforts have resulted in accidents or bodily harm, per the following table:

DOOR SLAMMED ON CLAIMANT'S FOOT	$ 1.00
FACE SLAPPED	1.00
EYE BLACKENED	2.00
CLAIMANT THROWN DOWN STAIRS BY GIRL FRIEND'S FATHER	3.00
CLAIMANT THROWN DOWN STAIRS BY GIRL FRIEND'S HUSBAND	5.00
CLAIMANT THROWN DOWN STAIRS BY GIRL FRIEND	10.00

NEW POTRZEBIE

INSURANCE CO.
New York
London Paris Rome Xanadu

Draft

INSURANCE

This Policy guarantees

COMPENSATION

for drafted males between
the ages of 18 and 21, per
stipulations hereinafter
stated—to wit: payment of
a cash sum to the draftee,
plus one fruit cake pack-
age on every other Friday.

FAITH   HOPE

DUPLICITY

This policy and all its provisions shall not apply to
anyone over three feet tall, weighing less than 300 lbs.

MUTUAL DISTRUST UNDERWRITERS CO.

★ ★ ★ ★ ★ ★ ★ ★ ★

No. 50 - 666 - B714 - M

ALLOWANCE

PROTECTION PLAN

SUBJECT TO PREMIUM CHARGES
STATED HEREIN, THIS POLICY
INSURED CLAIMANT AGAINST
ACCIDENTAL SHORTAGES
OF ALLOWANCE AND/OR OTHER
TEMPORARY ABSENCES OF READY

CASH

★ ★ ★ ★ ★ ★ ★ ★ ★

"Mutual Distrust"
Found the World Over

The Crudential Insurace Co. Gibraltar, N.J.

J I L T

INSURANCE

This policy insures claimant against unexpected jilting by member of the opposite sex.

Extended coverage (optional, see Par. 64-c) provides extra compensation for Saturday night "no-shows" and non-return of class or frat pin.

Policy Number --432-K

END

AND THEN I RE-WROTE DEPT.

Whenever we see one of those hour-long TV dramas, we're thankful that there's a place where people can see the works of talented American writers performed as they were written! Namely, Broadway! Because most TV dramas these days are pretty sad! In fact, we've often wondered what happens to a TV script once the writer turns it in. Recently, a network spy sent us the following material from a play to be presented on the Gloober Playhouse which clearly shows

How A Television Script Is Born

Here is the
original script
as it was first
written by the
Author, who has
also included
his personal
comments:

In this play, I show how it is possible for a boy to have all the benefits of a good home, and still feel unwanted. The first scene shows how Sidney's father, a judge, is too involved in courtroom work to pay attention to his son.

Johnny's coming by, Dad! Is it okay if we go for a ride in the car?

Do what you like, Sidney!

Don't bother your father when he's working on his courtroom cases!

This next scene shows Sidney's feelings toward his father . . . his resentment at being ignored. This lack of companionship between father and son is really what drives Sidney into seeking the friendship of a mixed-up boy like Johnny.

Did your old man say we could use his car, Sid?

Sure! He's too busy to care *what* I do!

Then let's go! I know a great stretch where we can really open 'er up, man!

Goaded by Johnny, Sidney drives wildly through town until he accidentally strikes down a dog. He is immediately sorry for what he has done, but lacks the moral fiber to stop and face the dog's owner, so he speeds away from the scene.

Let's go, man! Let's get out of here!

They killed my dog! But I'll track them down! I got the license number of that Cadillac . . .

This scene depicts Sidney's moment of manhood. We see that he is basically a responsible person when he confesses what has happened to the judge. We also see the judge's moment of truth when he realizes his own failings as a father.

Confronted by the dog's owner, the judge faces a difficult decision. As a father, he is guilty of neglecting his son. But as a judge, he must be impartial. He decides, therefore, to bring the actions of his son (and himself) to trial.

From the Author, the script then went to the Script Editor of the program who made the following changes and comments:

This is a fine script! Let's not touch a thing! Except . . . how many boys have fathers who are judges? One out of 5000? That's why I've made the old man a professional golfer. My old man was a professional golfer, and he ignored me!

May I go out with John tonight, Dad? We're going to strip down a car engine!

Sure, sure . . . only don't interrupt when I'm *putting!* .

Have fun, dear!

Nothing to be changed here, except I don't feel we should sympathize with the boy too much. So I've made him a mechanical genius, an egghead. That way it really isn't so much the old man's fault. I know! I've got an egghead for a son!

Is it okay for you to go out, Sid?

Sure! He's too involved in his *golf* to care what I do!

Swell! I've spotted a keen *Jag* we can strip down ...

Note that I've changed the Caddy to a Jaguar here. I own a Jag myself, and I **know** how keen they are! Also note that I've eliminated the dog-killing. Those A. S. P. C. A. phone calls can be murder, so why go **looking** for trouble?

Too bad the *owner* had to show up before we got it back together ...

I'll track down those boys! One of them left his *wrench* ...

This scene is okay, except it misses the boat. Sidney's father isn't upset; in fact he's sort of pleased to find his kid is human, and isn't so perfect. After all, that's the way I'd act if it happened to that smart-aleck kid of mine.

This scene lacked warmth, so I've fixed it. By offering to buy Sidney his own Jaguar, the old man turns out to be a swell guy, and everybody is happy, which always makes a good ending. I know it's the kind of ending my family'd like.

From the
Script Editor,
the play then went
to the Advertising
Agency TV Director
who read it and
made these
changes:

Scriptwise, this play is great. But I was just a little bothered by the father, so I've eliminated him. I've also changed the boy's name from Sidney to Steve—sounds more **American**. We can't afford to offend the American Legion!

Hey, Mom! Can I go out and play baseball?

Of course, Steve! You've been *helping* me all day . . .

Note that Steve and his friend, Bill (the name "John" is distasteful, reminds people of John Wilkes Booth!), are no longer **boy mechanics**. The **real** mechanics in the country might be offended, and we don't want to appear **anti-union**.

It is okay for you to play ball, Steve?

Sure, Bill! The only thing I hate is leaving Mom *alone!*

Bring your ball. The gang's waitin' in the lot by the highway!

I've rewritten here so the boys play **baseball**. This agency is also handling the Major League telecasts this season, so we might as well get in a plug where we can. I've also changed the car to a **Ford**. It might help land the account.

Boy! You really swatted that one, Steve! Too bad it smashed that Ford's windshield!

I'll track down those boys! One of them owns this *ball!*

No changes! I just want to point out that by eliminating the father, it means the boy lives alone with his mother, she takes in laundry, they're hard up, and she cries a lot. It keeps the audience in a sober mood for commercials.

...and we ran away! I...I had to tell you, Mom!

Oh, Steve! What am I going to do with... what's that? Someone's at the door? It's the owner of the Ford! How will we ever get the money to pay for the windshield?

This scene lacked real emotion, so I fixed it. Since every American boy dreams of becoming a Big League ball player so he can make lots of money and help his old sick mother, let's have the car-owner turn out to be a Baseball Scout.

Yes, I'm the one who hit your windshield with the ball! I'm sorry...

I'm not sorry, son! You're a natural hitter! And I happen to be a scout for the Yankees! Just sign this bonus contract!

Oh, Steve, now we can have all the things we ever wanted!

From the Ad Agency TV Director, the script was turned in to the Sponsor who had his own thoughts and made these changes:

This is a fine play. However, may I remind you that it's sponsored by Gloober's Breadcrumbs, not Baseball. Since Gloober's Breadcrumbs are used by women, I've made the central character a girl, naming her Maxine, after my daughter.

Ma, I'm going to the Rock 'n Roll show with Gladys!

A girl your age should be thinking of *marriage* instead of Rock 'n Roll.

Note my new emphasis on Rock 'n Roll. I think this is important for product-exposure. Teenagers are potential Breadcrumb-buyers, so if we tie the two together in their minds, they'll buy Gloober's Breadcrumbs when they **grow up.**

Ready to go, Maxine?

Ready! Hope we can get in!

Bring your *autograph book!* We'll wait at the Stage Door for Jerry Lee Lummox's personal autograph!

I'm glad I could eliminate the baseball scenes. This new backstage scene gives all the viewers a chance to see Dicky Finster, my daughter's favorite entertainer, who I suggest be cast as the singer so my daughter can get to **meet** him.

Isn't he *devine?* Isn't he *cool* and *crazy?*

Hey, some girl dropped her autograph book! Maybe her *name* is inside and I can track her down!

I've tinkered here. By having the girl cry, we give the mother a chance to do something else while she comforts her, like opening a box of Gloober's Breadcrumb Mix. Note, the close-ups I've indicated, shooting past the Gloober box.

Will you stop crying over loosing a silly autograph book and start thinking about getting *married!*

I *can't!* Jerry Lee Lummox is *my whole* life!

Someone's at the door! Stop sniveling and see who it is!

The last scene has everything—now. It brings the boy and girl together, it gives Dicky-boy a chance to sing another song, and mainly, it gives the mother more time to show off some of her tasty-looking Gloober's Breadcrumb recipes.

It's *you!* It's *really you!*

I found your ...say, you're pretty *cute!*

Such a *nice* man! You must stay for *dinner* and have some of my Gloober's Breadcrumb Pizza!

From the Sponsor, the script was then sent to a Network Vice-President who put the finishing touches on this final version:

Since Rock 'n Roll might offend **parents**, I've changed the stage show to a fancy costume ball. By replacing the girl friend with a godmother, we add **family interest**, and also create a part for Daphne Rancid, who's under contract to us.

Why are you so sad, my Dear?

Oh, Godmother! I wish *I* could go to the ball!

Is *that* all? Well, *we'll* fix that...

I don't mean to be difficult, but an autograph book doesn't make much sense at a costume ball. I changed it so she loses her slipper instead. And having the girl (I've named her Cindy) due home by midnight injects some needed suspense.

The clock tolls *midnight!* I must leave! I *must*...

That girl! How will I ever *find* her again? Ah, she dropped her *slipper!*

Since this is a touchy script, let's avoid all objections by changing the time to the Middle Ages. And let's soft-pedal the sponsor's plugs! After all, we could ruin this really great play by following everybody's two-bit suggestions.

And the Prince is searching for the girl who dropped the slipper! He wants to *marry* her!

Don't just *sit* there, Cindy! Answer the door! It must be the P R I N C E !

A few minor alterations in plot, characterization and dialogue, and the show wraps up just beautifully. The critics should love it. This is the kind of fresh new writing TV needs! The author should be encouraged to do more for us!

The slipper *fits!* I've found you at last! Marry me! I love you!

And I love you!

END

In the good old days, people either bought their books in a store, or swiped them from their friends. Today, more and more people are building their libraries by joining monthly book clubs. At last count, there were more than a dozen of these book clubs, each one trying to outdo the other to gain members. To accomplish this, many book clubs were specializing. So now, in an effort to win the heartfelt hatred of the book industry . . .

MAD LOOKS AT BOOK CLUBS

"Hey" "Heidi"

All in one eye-opening volume...when you join

THE SPICY ABRIDGED BOOK CLUB

Now you don't have to thumb through books anymore, looking for the "choicest parts." THE SPICY ABRIDGED BOOK CLUB sends you books containing only them "choicest parts". Every month, our board of judges—12 enlisted men at Fort Dix—submit hundreds of underlined paragraphs from books they've read. We, in turn, compile these into one SPICY ABRIDGED BOOK and offer it exclusively to our beady-eyed members.

Start Your Membership Now
CHOOSE ANY ONE
OF THESE
JUICY SELECTIONS

The SPICY ABRIDGED Erskine Caldwell

Over 1000 choice paragraphs of sun-drenched excitement selected from his best books.

The SPICY ABRIDGED French Novel

The raciest parts of books by Balzac, Zola, Flaubert, De Maupassant and De Gaulle.

The SPICY ABRIDGED Mickey Spillane

A selection of the meatiest parts of his books, meaning every word he ever wrote!

135

Here's the opportunity you have been waiting for, the chance to build a library dealing with one of the most popular figures in American History — Millard Fillmore. In addition to a 20-Volume set of Fillmore's Collected Papers (some of which even have writing on them!), new members will also receive free a desk blotter bearing Fillmore's picture, plus a button from his unsuccessful bid for re-nomination in 1852 reading "I like Millard!"

Choose any one of these books as your first selection

1. MILLARD FILLMORE'S EARLY BOYHOOD Part I—Infancy to Age 2½, 655 Pages..$18.50
FILLMORE'S FAVORITE DINNER MENUS—1850-1852, 705 Pages $21.00
THE DAY MILLARD FILLMORE DIDN'T SHAVE by Jim Bishop, 1,100 Pages.....$30.00
WHO IN HECK WAS MILLARD FILLMORE ANYHOW? By Benj. Harrison, 1 Page. $50.00

****

MILLARD FILLMORE BOOK CLUB,
Deathly, Ill.

Please enroll me in THE MILLARD FILLMORE BOOK CLUB, and send my first selection. I understand that when I become a member, I will be sent the FREE 20-Volume set of "The Collected Papers of Millard Fillmore". I also understand that I don't become a member until I have purchased 36 consecutive monthly selections at prices ranging from $18.50 to $50.00. I further understand that if I miss a single month I am obligated to start all over again

As my first selection, send me: _____

NAME _____

ADDRESS _____

CITY _____ STATE _____

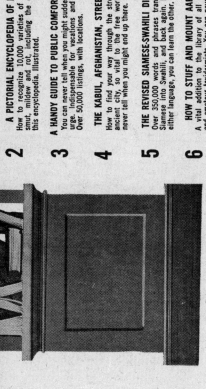

2

A PICTORIAL ENCYCLOPEDIA OF FUNGUS

How to recognize 10,000 varieties of rust, mold, smut, mildew and rot, including the contents of this encyclopedia. Illustrated. 600 pages.

3

A HANDY GUIDE TO PUBLIC COMFORT STATIONS

You can never tell when you might suddenly have the urge. Indispensable for vacations and long trips. Over 50,000 listings, with locations. 987 pages.

4

THE KABUL, AFGHANISTAN, STREET GUIDE

How to find your way through the streets of this ancient city, so vital to the free world. You can never tell when you might end up there. 4 pages.

5

THE REVISED SIAMESE-SWAHILI DICTIONARY

Over 350,000 words and phrases translated from Siamese into Swahili, and back again. If you know either language, you can learn the other. 10 pages.

6

HOW TO STUFF AND MOUNT AARDVARKS

A vital addition to the library of all professional and amateur taxidermists. You can never tell when some clown will walk in with one of these monsters.

THE USEFUL INFORMATION BOOK CLUB

I want to join the USEFUL INFORMATION BOOK CLUB, because I want to gather all the useful information I can while I am alive, so I'll be pretty smart when I'm dead. Please enroll me and send my 3-book bonus offer. I understand that when I join, I promise to purchase 10 out of the 12 USEFUL INFORMATION books selected during the next year. Now, here's some USEFUL INFORMATION for you. Mainly, if I were you guys, I wouldn't trust me to do that!

NAMES OF 3 BOOKS SELECTED _____

MY NAME IS: _____

MY ADDRESS IS: _____

MY CITY IS: _____ MY STATE IS: _____

THE
RIDICULOUSLY-EXPENSIVE *Book Club*

Yes, now you can own the costliest, most ornate editions of the great classics of world literature. Each volume is printed on imported Norwegian parchment, coated with an authentic layer of 200-year-old dust. Each hand-pressed binding is made of leather taken from the backside of an East African gazelle. Each line of type has been hand-set by expert Westphalian craftsmen. And each page is uncut, because these books are for showing off, not for reading!

▶ start your membership now with one of these RIDICULOUSLY-EXPENSIVE BOOKS!

BLACK BEAUTY

A luxurious binding embossed with pure gold excavated from the burial vault of the Aztec temple of Tehuantepec. Stitched with thread from Cleopatra's original bridal veil, using her own needle.

THE ROVER BOYS

An unimaginably-expensive binding studded with emeralds from the crown of Queen Isabella of Spain. Also comes with a rare 10-inch bookmark made from the tongue of a yearling Bolivian milk-fed vicuña.

WINNIE THE POOH

Ultra-lavish binding inlaid with silver taken from the teeth fillings of Marie Antoinette, and studded with 10 rubies brought from Cathay by Marco Polo. Cover painted with oils left over by Rembrandt.

TRICK-OR-CHEAT DEPT.

There is nothing more infectious and exciting than the shouting and yelling and hollering and screaming of people enjoying a Sport, whether it be Baseball or Football or Basketball or Pin-the-tail-on-the-donkey. And so, with this thought in mind, we now turn the MAD spotlight on the one Sport that can boast of more shouting and yelling and hollering and screaming than any other sport . . . namely

♠ ♦ BRIDGE ♥ ♣

MOST BRIDGE PLAYERS HAVE A CASUA
MERELY CONSIDER IT A PLEASANT WAY

♥ ♣
THE ARISTOCRAT
OF CARD GAMES
♠ ♦

ATTITUDE TOWARD THE GAME, AND
TO SOCIALIZE WITH THEIR FRIENDS.

A GLOSSARY OF BRIDGE TERMS

DUMMY

Every partner you have in Bridge, be it wife. husband, friend or relative.

WEAK RESPONSE

Partner's hand is not strong enough to withstand forcing bid, *passes . . . out.*

POINT COUNT

Player *points* out and *counts* number of times partner played like an imbecile.

FINESSE

Player signaling partner does it with finesse so opponents don't catch wise

DOUBLING

Player gets hysterical over opponent's
stupid play, *doubles up* with laughter.

REDOUBLING

Opponent resents doubling first player is doing, and so he *redoubles* him.

CALLING BID

Player *calls* other player's bid what
he thinks of it, usually followed by

OVERCALLING BID

All four players get into act and *call*
what they think of the other's bidding.

LITTLE SLAM

Player, disgusted with hand dealt him,
loses temper and *slams* cards on table.

GRAND SLAM

Rest of players, disgusted with hands,
themselves, and Bridge, lose tempers

FORCING BID

A player with a good hand informs his partner that a response is *mandatory*.

VULNERABLE

Player is overly-sensitive and *breaks down* over comments about her playing.

YOU CAN LEARN A LOT ABOUT BRIDGE BY FOLLOWING THE MANY COLUMNS IN NEWSPAPERS AND MAGAZINES DEVOTED TO THIS FASCINATING GAME. HERE IS A TYPICAL EXAMPLE, WRITTEN BY THE LEADING EXPERT IN THE FIELD . . .

CHARLES GROAN / CARDS

Separating Suits

Neither side friendly
North dealer

NORTH

NORTH	EAST	SOUTH	WEST	NORTHWEST
1 ♣	2 ♥	3 ♦	4 ♣	5 KIBITZ
5 WHAT? 5 KIBITZ?	WHO'S THE WISE GUY?	NOT ME! IT'S HIM!	WILL YOU SHUT UP!	MAKE ME!
SOMEBODY SOCK HIM!	PASS!	PASS!	PASS!	YOU'RE ALL YELLOW!
OH, YEAH! PUT 'EM UP!	POW!	SOCK!	GRUNT!	THUD!

Opening lead: right uppercut

Here is a perfect example of the effectiveness of "separating suits" when it comes to Bridge. I couldn't help hearing about this hand as it was going on, so I rushed next door to enjoy it.

West opened the heart queen, dummy covered, and East sneezed, scattering dummy's cards over the floor. Then she played the king. Dummy took the trick with her hand. West called a *renege*, pointing out that declarer hadn't played a card. Declarer called West a sore-loser and played the ace. Then she set up her club suit by leading the king, forcing West's ace. Dummy played low, since the cards were still on the floor, and East trumped with the spade 5. West did a double-take and asked to see the trick, pointing out that East had just pulled the bone-head play of the century, trumping her partner's ace. Bonehead wasn't exactly East's favorite nickname, so she threw a small diamond to the table. But West managed to talk her into putting it back on her finger, and East led a spade, pulling West's only trump. West then screamed that his heart-lead had indicated a singleton, and if East had any brains, she'd have led a heart so he could use his only trump to win a trick. So East promptly led a small club, right over West's head!

Meanwhile, South took the trick with her ace, continued extracting trump, and ended up in dummy. Whereupon her husband exploded, pointing out that now she couldn't run the club suit because she couldn't get back to her hand. So South gave him the back to her hand, and showed him! Right across the mouth!

The score was then found to be inaccurate, and everybody decided to call it an evening. In fact, they decided to call it a friendship!

The forthcoming marriage between East and West was cancelled, but not before an ugly court wrangle! The three-year-old marriage between North and South was ended in a quickie Mexican Divorce! And there you have the effectiveness of "separating suits"!

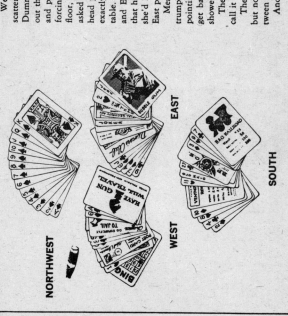

NORTHWEST

EAST

WEST

SOUTH

LIKE WE SAID, BRIDGE IS A PLEASANT
FRIENDS YOU CAN'T STAND AND WANT

END

The Army, the Navy and the Air Force all hand out medals for Heroic Military Achievements, but there is no organization to hand out medals for Heroic Civilian Achievements. And some

MAD MEDALS

THE FEARLESS AND

AWARDED TO

Zelda Zitzlaff

Housewife

of Taft-Hartley, Vt.

FOR

DECISIVE ASSAULT

On April 8th, 1959, Mrs. Zitzlaff took delivery on a new sofa, and when the men left, immediately removed the "Do Not Remove Tags" from the cushions.

the Civilian Achievements we got in mind make them Mili-
ry Achievements look like child's play. You'll see what we
ean when you read the citations that accompany these . . .

FOR EVERYDAY HEROES

INDEPENDENT ACTION MEDAL

THE HEROISM ON

AWARDED TO

Fenwick J. Finster
Salesman
of Ho-Fo-Kus, N.J.
FOR
VALIANT
SELF-CONTROL

On June 21st, 1959, Mr.
Finster dragged out his
lights and equipment and
took "home movies" of his
wife and children without
once losing his temper

THE HOME FRONT MEDAL

THE DISPOSAL OF HIDDEN

AWARDED TO

Arthur L. Mudge
Itinerant
of Sleeping Car, N.C.

FOR

EFFICIENT
DEXTERITY

On June 17th, 1959, Mr. Mudge, having purchased a brand new shirt, located and removed every one of them carefully concealed pins before putting it on.

BOOBY TRAPS MEDAL

THE VICTORY OVER

AWARDED TO

Fanny Strongthumber

Housewife

of Mangle, Maine

FOR

DISTINGUISHED ACHIEVEMENT

On June 6th, 1959, Mrs. Strongthumber succeeded in tearing open a typical cellophane-wrapped bag of potato chips without having once used her teeth.

MODERN PACKAGING MEDAI

THE EXECUTION OF

AWARDED TO

Freda Prawn
Housewife
of Pumpspout, Ga.
FOR
DETERMINATION
UNDER FIRE

On May 27th, 1959, Mrs. Prawn traveled to a local supermarket, and made her weekly purchases without buying one item that was not on her shopping list.

PLANNED STRATEGY MEDAL

THE TRIUMPH OVER

AWARDED TO

Elihu Bunchwell
Housepainter
of Kemtone, Neb.

FOR

MERITORIOUS SERVICE

On April 4th, 1959 Mr. Bunchwell spread his dropcloth, and, on the very first try, mixed up the exact shade of chartreuse a woman-customer wanted.

IMPOSSIBLE ODDS MEDAL

END

TIME was when a serious writer struggled and sweated to turn out a good book, only to find when it was published that six people bought it. So the poor shnook ended up with maybe $3.00 in royalties and a dog-eared collection of mouldy reviews.

But not any more! Nowadays, a serious writer turns out

A Best Seller

YOU RAVED ABOUT THE BOOK...

...NOW SEE THE PLAY!

"Hypnotising!" "A Smash!"
Svengali,   Butterfingers,
N. Y. Times   Crockery Journal

BORIS PASTERNAK'S
NEW DRAMA

COME BACK LITTLE DOCTOR

with

SHIRLEY PHONEBOOTH & SIDNEY BLACKOUT

Directed by ELIA FEELYA

Mon. thru Thurs. Eves. Orch. $6.90; Bal. $5.75, 4.80, 3.60, Fri.-& Sat. Eves. Orch. $7.50; Bal., $6.90, 5.75, 4.80, 3.60, 3.

ALFRED E. NEUMAN THEATRE
44 Street West Off-Broadway

a good book and — before you can say "Ernest Hemingway!" — they turn him into a "corporation." Then he has to be a play-producer, merchandiser—even a stock market operator. Because nowadays, literature is *big business!*

Take f'rinstance the current best-seller on the left — a serious-type novel about the Russian Revolution called "Doctor Zhivago." Let's follow (at a safe distance) and see what happens when . . .

Hits The

COMMERCIAL

TRAIL

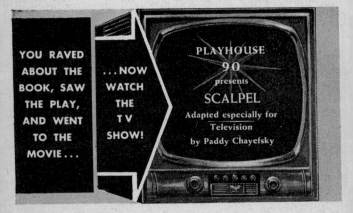

YOU RAVED ABOUT THE BOOK, SAW THE PLAY, AND WENT TO THE MOVIE...

...NOW WATCH THE T V SHOW!

PLAYHOUSE 90 presents SCALPEL Adapted especially for Television by Paddy Chayefsky

YOU RAVED ABOUT THE BOOK, SAW THE PLAY, WENT TO THE MOVIE, WATCHED THE TV SHOW, ENJOYED THE MUSICAL, AND BOUGHT THE RECORD . . .

. . . NOW LISTEN TO THE RADIO SERIAL!

Will Anna Ivanova marry Colonel Kavkhaztsev? Will Pasha and Larisa Antipov find lasting happiness in Nishni-Novgorod? Tune in tomorrow . . . When Diamond Crystal Siberian Salt presents the next exciting episode of "DOCTOR ZHIVAGO FACES LIFE"

YOU RAVED ABOUT THE BOOK, SAW THE PLAY, WENT TO THE MOVIE, WATCHED THE TV SHOW, ENJOYED THE MUSICAL, BOUGHT THE RECORD, AND LISTENED TO THE RADIO SERIAL . . . . . . NOW FOLLOW THE COMIC STRIP!

YOU RAVED ABOUT THE BOOK, SAW THE PLAY, WENT TO THE MOVIE, WATCHED THE TV SHOW, ENJOYED THE MUSICAL, BOUGHT THE RECORD, LISTENED TO THE RADIO SERIAL, AND FOLLOWED THE COMIC STRIP...

...NOW WEAR THE HAT!

YOU RAVED ABOUT THE BOOK, SAW THE PLAY, WENT TO THE MOVIE, WATCHED THE TV SHOW, ENJOYED THE MUSICAL, BOUGHT THE RECORD, LISTENED TO THE RADIO SERIAL, FOLLOWED THE COMIC STRIP, AND WORE THE HAT . . .

. . . NOW BUY THE DOLL!

THE ORIGINAL "DOCTOR ZHIVAGO" DOLL

It Talks—
It Walks—
It Wets—
It Spies—

YOU RAVED ABOUT THE BOOK, SAW THE PLAY, WENT TO THE MOVIE, WATCHED THE TV SHOW, ENJOYED THE MUSICAL, BOUGHT THE RECORD, LISTENED TO THE RADIO SERIAL, FOLLOWED THE COMIC STRIP, WORE THE HAT, AND BOUGHT THE DOLL . . .

...NOW GET THE COCKTAIL NAPKINS!

YOU RAVED ABOUT THE BOOK, SAW THE PLAY, WENT TO THE MOVIE, WATCHED THE TV SHOW, ENJOYED THE MUSICAL, BOUGHT THE RECORD, LISTENED TO THE RADIO SERIAL, FOLLOWED THE COMIC STRIP, WORE THE HAT, BOUGHT THE DOLL, GOT THE COCKTAIL NAPKINS, AND SMOKED THE CIGARETTES . . .

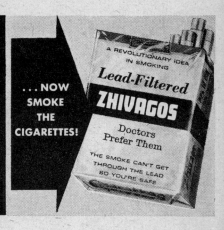

YOU RAVED ABOUT THE BOOK, SAW THE PLAY, WENT TO THE MOVIE, WATCHED THE TV SHOW, ENJOYED THE MUSICAL, BOUGHT THE RECORD, LISTENED TO THE RADIO SERIAL, FOLLOWED THE COMIC STRIP, WORE THE HAT, BOUGHT THE DOLL, AND GOT THE COCKTAIL NAPKINS . . .

. . . NOW SMOKE THE CIGARETTES!

A REVOLUTIONARY IDEA IN SMOKING

Lead-Filtered

ZHIVAGOS

Doctors Prefer Them

THE SMOKE CAN'T GET THROUGH THE LEAD SO YOU'RE SAFE

. . . NOW WORK THE JIGSAW PUZZLE!

YOU RAVED ABOUT THE
BOOK, SAW THE PLAY,
WENT TO THE MOVIE,
WATCHED THE TV SHOW,
ENJOYED THE MUSICAL,
BOUGHT THE RECORD,
LISTENED TO THE RADIO
SERIAL, FOLLOWED THE
COMIC STRIP, WORE THE
HAT, BOUGHT THE DOLL,
GOT THE COCKTAIL NAPKINS,
SMOKED THE CIGARETTES,
AND WORKED THE JIGSAW
PUZZLE . . .

. . . NOW
SAVE THE
BUBBLE-GUM
CARDS!

DOCTOR ZHIVAGO CARD NO. 1

Taking a Tramp Through the Snow

When he was sixteen, Yura Zhivago went to Pirogen University to study medicine. In his spare time, he enjoyed taking a tramp through the snow. The tramp, whose name was Sascha, also enjoyed these romps.

YOU RAVED ABOUT THE BOOK, SAW THE PLAY, WENT TO THE MOVIE, WATCHED THE TV SHOW, ENJOYED THE MUSICAL, BOUGHT THE RECORD, LISTENED TO THE RADIO SERIAL, FOLLOWED THE COMIC STRIP, WORE THE HAT, BOUGHT THE DOLL, GOT THE COCKTAIL NAPKINS, SMOKED THE CIGARETTES, WORKED THE JIGSAW PUZZLE, AND SAVED THE BUBBLE-GUM CARDS . . .

. . . NOW BUY THE BOOK AND **READ IT,** ALREADY!

END

FACE VALUE DEPT.

If you're a fella, you probably have a good idea what you look like from staring into your bathroom mirror while shaving. (And if you're a girl, you probably have a good idea what you look like from staring into your compact mirror while shaving.) But the truth is . . . other people see you a lot differently than you see yourself. Because people who know you have their own way of recognizing you. So, with this article, MAD shows . . .

How You Look to Other People

HOW YOU LOOK TO
YOUR TEACHER

HOW YOU LOOK TO YOUR NEWSDEALER

HOW YOU LOOK TO YOUR DENTIST

HOW YOU LOOK TO YOUR WAITRESS

HOW YOU LOOK TO YOUR LAWYER

HOW YOU LOOK TO
YOUR DOCTOR

HOW YOU LOOK TO
YOUR BOSS

HOW YOU LOOK TO
YOUR FIANCEE

HOW YOU LOOK TO
YOUR POSTMAN

HOW YOU LOOK TO
YOUR CLERGYMAN

HOW YOU LOOK TO
YOUR WIFE

HOW YOU LOOK TO
YOUR MANICURIST

HOW YOU LOOK TO
YOUR BARBER

END

Don Martin's art experiences are many and varied
. . . for instance the time he observed the creative
effort of

THE
SCULPTOR
IN HIS
STUDIO

END